A Century of Iowa Architecture

1900–1999

Celebrating 100 Years • Promoting Design Excellence in Iowa • 1904-2004

In 1904, eight architects in Des Moines elected to form a subgroup of the American Institute of Architects. Today, more than 650 members belong to the American Institute of Architects, Iowa Chapter (AIA Iowa). AIA Iowa is an individual membership organization consisting of registered architects; those architecturally trained, but not registered; technical personnel employed by architects; affiliated design professionals; and service and supply providers allied to the architectural field. In forwarding our mission of "Improving the built environment through service to members, the profession and the public," the chapter provides outreach and public relations, legislative advocacy and continuing education services for its members.

AIA—Building On Your Vision *www.aiaiowa.org*

ISBN 0-9761814-0-1

Design by Mauck+Associates

A Century of Iowa Architecture was made possible
by the generous contributions of the following:

  Members of AIA Iowa
  CNA Insurance Companies
  Victor O. Schinnerer & Company
  The AIA Trust
  Pella Rolscreen Foundation
  Iowa Architectural Foundation

CONTENTS

INTRODUCTION

Iowa is known as the prehistoric home of the Mound Builders, Native American tribes that constructed ceremonial mounds throughout the state. It's obvious that there was a strong desire from thousands of years ago to make an enduring mark on the land, and this has been a repeated pattern with each successive group of people who have come to populate the state. The reasons for the early interest in Iowa are clear; some of the best agricultural soil in the world is here. This is combined with open rolling prairie that required little clearing, abundant fingers of timber along navigable waterways and ample supplies of coal and limestone. Establishing towns and farmsteads in Iowa occurred at a very rapid pace because of these resources which contributed to a particular way of building here. Most of the state's buildings from early on reflect a keen understanding of contemporary building technique and style, combined with a Midwestern ethic for making things uncommonly well.

The people of Iowa are known as hardworking and well-educated; early communities typically constructed a school as the first public building, establishing Iowa for a long period as the most literate state in the nation. By the end of the 19th century, most moderately populated communities included practicing architects; their influence is seen in the quality of the structures throughout the 20th century. The communities that built the towns also were very progressive; the common belief that cultured ideas moved slowly through the state from east to west is not supported by reviewing the buildings. Looking at the range of projects shown here is fascinating and illustrates the extraordinary growth of Iowa during the previous century, with concentrations of noteworthy buildings revealing the prosperity of towns during a particular time.

The projects illustrated in this book were selected from nominations that were juried by a panel of distinguished Iowans (see Acknowledgements). In selecting the projects to be honored, the jury was careful to consider issues related to the buildings' civic and cultural significance in addition to design excellence. The buildings represented here are an attempt to celebrate a small portion of Iowa's exceptional architecture and the high quality of the communities that created it.

1900–1909

The first decade of the 20th century shows the heavy influence of 19th-century neoclassical Beaux Arts style in Iowa town planning and the design of civic structures. Many towns and cities had firmly established themselves by this time and were rebuilding public structures more substantially and at a larger scale than their original municipal buildings.

At the beginning of the 1900s, public commissions were increasingly done by Iowa architects rather than firms from out of state. Town planning and growth was inspired by the City Beautiful Movement, a Beaux Arts style of planning begun in Chicago at the World's Columbian Exposition of 1893. Many of Iowa's towns began the process of constructing downtown squares and civic centers with linked parks and tree-lined boulevards in response to visiting the Exposition. Evidence of these projects is seen throughout the state, most notably in Des Moines, Cedar Rapids and Davenport.

During this decade, an early shift is seen first in residential design and later in public buildings with the arrival of the Arts and Crafts style and the growing influence of Frank Lloyd Wright and the Prairie School of design. However, when constructing government buildings, neoclassical styles were still the norm, as they were able to borrow the language and legitimacy of age-old European civic structures. Majestic examples can be seen in the Polk County Courthouse and the Des Moines Public Library, but more modest examples are evident throughout the state in the splendid Carnegie libraries such as the Kendall Young Library in Webster City.

1910–1919

The early influences of the Prairie School seen in the previous decade are more fully realized during the time between 1910 and 1919. The financial productivity of the state is evident as pockets of wealth emerge and are reflected in towns such as Mason City, which features the entire neighborhood of Rock Crest/Rock Glen on the National Historic Register. Frank Lloyd Wright's Stockman residence, along with a series of amazing homes by Walter Burley Griffin, is located here, placing it among the most significant Prairie School areas in the nation.

Louis Sullivan's influence out of Chicago is often seen, as buildings shift away from traditional Beaux Arts design and toward more contemporary thinking. Much of this change is due to new building technologies; there is a desire to reflect the modern era in the buildings rather than borrow styles from a time and culture more distant from the rapidly changing world of technological revolution. Sullivan also abstracts and enriches the notion of architectural ornamentation in remarkable buildings like Grinnell's Merchants National Bank.

The myth that ideas spread slowly from east to west in the state is effectively dispelled by the Woodbury County Courthouse, a magnificently progressive Prairie School building on the western edge of Iowa in Sioux City.

1920–1929

The prosperity of the 1920s is reflected in the grand homes and large-scale public buildings constructed during this era. There is a return over the course of the decade to the neoclassical styles, as the Prairie School buildings were more austere and less expressive of the national affluence.

The prevalence of steel construction changed the way tall buildings were built and expressed. Without the need to have heavy masonry bearing walls, the buildings soared to new heights yet could maintain a more delicate, slender structural expression. This can be seen in projects like the First National Bank in Davenport and the Equitable Building in Des Moines. The style of many of these buildings shows a simplification of Beaux Arts design and a mixture of traditional elements blended together.

Art Deco and International Style modernist structures were becoming more common in Europe, but this style of building had yet to gain wide acceptance in the United States. In contrast, large homes were built in the style of English country manors, such as the impressive Salisbury House in Des Moines constructed by the Weeks family. Here we see a strong desire to express a connection to English noble life, with elements of the building actually taken from 16th-century English buildings.

By the end of the decade there is a clear desire to represent many buildings in a more modern fashion, yet a true break with tradition would wait until the 1930s.

1930–1939

During the 1930s, we see the emergence of Art Deco as the expression of modern buildings. This style was taken from the 1925 Paris Exposition of Arts Decoratifs, and relied on geometric figures and a streamlined look reminiscent of modern planes and automobiles. There were many variations on the Art Deco approach, from the exuberant depiction of Native American figures on Sioux City's Badgerow Building to the much more austere expression of the Iowa-Des Moines National Bank Building.

The most modern examples of the style are seen in Sioux City's Grandview Park Band Shell and the stunning Butler House on the south side of Des Moines. In 1937, Ernest Clarke referred to the Butler House as "the world's most modern house," for both its streamlined, avant-garde styling and its extensive use of modern technologies, such as reinforced concrete construction and electric eyes that would automatically open garage doors.

The influence of the Prairie School is still seen in the 1930s with the large-scale design of Eagle Point Park Shelters in Dubuque. Here the landscape design and the numerous pavilions blend together in one of the finest expressions of "organic" design found in the country.

Building projects slowed dramatically toward the end of the decade due to the Great Depression; many significant projects would be on hold until after World War II.

1940–1949

The 1940s are defined by the pre- and post-World War II period. Before the war, lasting effects of the Great Depression resulted in halting most projects other than public works efforts, many funded as part of the Works Progress Administration. Eagle Point Park was funded in this way, as was the Julien Dubuque Bridge, a splendid example of elegant steel bridge construction.

Two projects that show a transition from the Art Deco style of the late 1930s to a more modern, unornamented style are Ventura's High School Auditorium and Gymnasium from 1940 and Burlington's Chicago, Burlington and Quincy railroad station of 1944. The auditorium and gymnasium exhibit many of the features of classic Art Deco ornamentation, with horizontal reliefs and geometric patterns on the exterior. The railroad station is a more restrained project with many of the features of International Style modernism, which would come to dominate the post-war period.

The latter part of the 1940s is represented by two projects from the internationally famous office of Eliel and Eero Saarinen. The Des Moines Art Center is an excellent example of a modern building integrating with the landscape, and was the catalyst for the development of a world-class museum complex. It is a masterfully conceived and executed project that enriches the community and is seen as one of the most significant buildings in the state. Fitch and Ingham Halls on the Drake University campus in Des Moines are simpler buildings that show a more direct relationship to European modern buildings such as Walter Gropius' famous Bauhaus school in Dessau, Germany.

World War II brought many of the best-known European architects and educators to the United States; their influence is strongly felt in the decades to come.

1950–1959

The postwar period of the 1950s sees a return of Frank Lloyd Wright to residential projects in Iowa. Wright is clearly the most famous American architect of all time, and had the uncanny ability to reinvent his way of working to create significant projects for more than half of the 20th century. The Walter House (Cedar Rock) in Quasqueton is a masterful example of Wright's Usonian style, with a central living core and a linear wing of private bedrooms. The Lamberson House in Oskaloosa is also in the Usonian style, with a characteristic low, horizontal roof reminiscent of the long, open stretches of Midwestern prairie and farmland Wright is responding to.

The middle of the decade is distinguished by further projects on the Drake campus; the most notable are Medbury Hall and the Oreon E. Scott Chapel by Eero Saarinen. The chapel is an understated simple brick cylinder from the outside yet powerfully dramatic on the interior, with exquisite detailing and a masterful use of natural light.

The end of the decade moves increasingly toward the influence of Mies van der Rohe with simple, minimal glass and steel structures such as the first home of Ray Crites in Cedar Rapids. The 1950s is a time of sweeping changes in modern design, and Iowa has particularly fine examples of this era of architecture.

1960–1969

The 1960s is the period of high modernism in Iowa and throughout the nation, with projects displaying ideals of honest expression in materials and building function. Ludwig Mies van der Rohe's Home Federal Savings and Loan Building in downtown Des Moines is a classic example of the glass-and-steel box, painstakingly detailed and lavished with granite and limestone interiors.

A block to the north is the American Republic Insurance Building—by Gordon Bunshaft of Skidmore, Owings & Merrill—a simple and elegant concrete structure with glass ends. This project expresses a clear diagram of the internal function displayed on the exterior: open offices on the upper floors, public space enclosed in glass below and entry/service functions housed in the concrete base. I. M. Pei completes the first addition to Saarinen's Des Moines Art Center with a concrete and glass sculpture wing designed to house larger-scale works being produced during the 1960s.

These are remarkable projects produced by internationally famous designers, but the most significant project of the decade, and judged to be the most important of the century, is C. Y. Stephens Auditorium at Iowa State University in Ames, designed by the Iowa firms of Crites & McConnell and Brooks Borg & Skiles Architects-Engineers. This project is not only beautifully assembled and functionally expressive, but also represents the efforts of the population to bring performing arts to central Iowa. This public gesture of investing in the cultural enrichment and education of the community, ideals intrinsic to the history of the state, is what elevates this project above all others to be considered the Building of the Century in Iowa.

1970–1979

In 1966 Robert Venturi wrote "Complexity and Contradiction in Architecture," his famous treatise on the need to rediscover meaning in buildings through the use of architecture's historic formal language. The first effects of questioning "modern architecture" are just beginning to be felt during the 1970s. Most of the early modernists believed in the power of design to change the world, but by the '70s it was difficult to maintain this degree of optimism. Nonetheless, the language of the projects in Iowa shows a refinement and exploration of the modernist kit of parts, rather than the changes seen in the decades to follow.

Concrete as both a cladding and structural material continues to be common, with forays into more expressive ways to use it, as in the large cantilevered roof of the Iowa Society of Christian Churches Building in Des Moines or the curved supports and walls in the Brenton Bank Building by Charles Herbert and Associates. Concrete volumes dramatically carved and extruded are seen in further work of Charles Herbert and Associates, both at the Blank Performing Arts Center at Simpson College in Indianola and the Civic Center of Greater Des Moines. The Civic Center was part of a larger project intended to give Des Moines a central focus by creating the performing arts building along with Nollen Plaza, which provides the city with a much-needed public gathering space. The ability to make the building a backdrop to the open plaza space was uncommon in modernist object structures, and shows an understanding of the need to defer to people as the most important component of any design.

1980-1989

The 1980s are widely known as the era of postmodernism, a movement critical of International Style modernism and interested in historical building references. This fashion of building fell out of favor quickly after the '80s, and while there are clear examples of this architecture in the state, a possible lingering distaste for the style has resulted in few buildings of this type being nominated and none selected. It is fair to say that postmodernism may be too whimsical and impractical to connect well with Iowa's common-sense attitude. In the projects shown we see modernism referenced from a less critical point of view, with elements taken from characteristic modern language and represented in different ways. Carver-Hawkeye Arena at the University of Iowa celebrates the need for a long-span structure by making it the dominant feature of the building exterior, while Richard Meier's addition to the Des Moines Art Center stays true to his typical manipulation of simple white porcelain-clad forms. The Agronomy Building at Iowa State University and the Des Moines Convention Center both use layered organizational systems with circulation celebrated as lighted glass corridors. The Convention Center by Brooks Borg & Skiles Architects-Engineers does a particularly fine job of expressing the shift between the grid of downtown streets and the rest of the city.

The only residential project featured since the 1950s, the Coppola residence by Douglas A. Wells Architect, is remarkable in its adherence to classic 1970's modern design principles. Building design in the 1980s shows the same steadiness of character and lack of interest in superfluous trends that has long distinguished the population of Iowa.

1990-1999

Recently completed buildings are difficult to place in historic context, and so the 1990s would appear to have a less consistent focus than the other decades. Elements of modernism are still very present as in the Forest Avenue Library and the Meredith Corporation Headquarters Expansion, both in Des Moines. These projects are elegantly detailed, well-conceived responses to their respective contexts. They also share a civic-minded motivation, with the library being the keystone of a major neighborhood revival and Meredith framing the development of downtown Des Moines' urban renewal project, Gateway West.

We also see references to postmodernism in the 801 Grand Building and the EMC Insurance Building, with gabled and arched forms at their peaks. The EMC building has a sophisticated cladding system that sheathes the tower, yet it meets the street with a surrounding colonnade that relates the building to a more human scale. 801 Grand is notable as the tallest building in the state and was certainly designed during the previous decade, with postmodern references to historic forms on the interior and exterior of the project. Frank O. Gehry and Associates designed the University of Iowa's Advanced Technology Laboratory, a group of warped and chaotic volumes characteristic of Gehry's work, undoubtedly the nation's most famous architect since Frank Lloyd Wright, creates projects more reminiscent of sculpture than buildings. The end of the 20th century in Iowa, as everywhere, does not represent a culmination but rather a continued search for what architecture is appropriate for its particular time and situation. These are the projects, respectfully submitted, deemed most successful at this difficult and heartfelt task.

1900

St. Paul's Episcopal Church
Harlan

A beautifully detailed church, it combines Queen Anne–Shingle, Gothic Revival and Arts and Crafts styles. The proportions and massing suggest a much larger building, but in person the scale is quite intimate.

Proudfoot & Bird

1903

Des Moines Public Library
Des Moines

The library was designed as part of a turn-of-the-century plan to develop the riverfront in Des Moines. It is an excellent example of Beaux Arts classical design with the large symmetrical entry portico leading to an impressive series of spaces within.

Smith & Gutterson

1905

Kendall Young Library
Webster City

This is one of the many fine Carnegie libraries located throughout Iowa. It is a richly detailed example of Beaux Arts design with the large pediment over the entry dominating the building.

Patton & Miller

**Building
of the
Decade**

1900–1909

1906

Polk County Courthouse
Des Moines

This large, beautifully proportioned Beaux Arts classical structure shows the great skill of the architects, Proudfoot & Bird. The tall clock tower is the east terminus of Court Avenue, balancing the State Capitol dome as the west terminus of Locust Street.

Proudfoot & Bird

1909

City National Bank Building/Park Inn Hotel
Mason City

This is a sophisticated example of Frank Lloyd Wright's ability to make complex functions blend together. It is an early example of a public building done in the Prairie Style.

Frank Lloyd Wright

1910

State Historical Memorial and Art Building
Des Moines

Begun before the turn of the century, this Beaux Arts design departs from the "standard" rules of classical architecture to create a unique and impressive building. The structure has recently been beautifully restored to much of its original glory.

Smith & Gutterson and Smith & Gage

1913

Masonic Temple
Des Moines

This brick and stone neoclassical design forms the
historic cornerstone of the Gateway West development
in Des Moines. The building has been successfully
renovated as a vibrant part of the downtown
revitalization.

Proudfoot Bird & Rawson

1914

Joshua G. Melson House
Mason City

This important house is part of the Rock Crest/Rock Glen development, famous for its Prairie Style homes and landscape design. The building dramatically overlooks the open park between the homes from a limestone outcropping.

Walter Burley Griffin Architect

**Building
of the
Decade**

1910–1919

1915

Merchants National Bank Building
Grinnell

One of Sullivan's most important bank buildings, virtually every architecture student in the country has studied it for over 70 years. The simple exterior box has a stunning terra-cotta entry and the interior is lit with a large stained glass side window and skylight.

Louis H. Sullivan

1918

Woodbury County Courthouse
Sioux City

The largest Prairie Style public building in Iowa, it is distinguished by a horizontal base with the tower above. The detailing is both intimate and meticulous. It is an example of an enlightened, community creating a modern public image.

William Steele and Purcell & Elmslie

1920

C. B. Baldwin House
Farson

The Prairie Style is rarely seen outside of the cities and suburbs, but this is a grand rural farmhouse done in this fashion. It is very formal in its arrangement and massing, reminiscent of Frank Lloyd Wright's Winslow House near Oak Park, Illinois.

G. M. Kerns

1922

Roosevelt High School
Des Moines

This school is designed in the fashion of a large 17th-century English home. The siting on the large grounds and stone detailing at the entry enhance the effect of viewing a country estate. This reverence for the place of education was typical of Iowa schools.

Proudfoot Bird & Rawson

1923

First National Bank Building
Davenport

This is a classic example of base, shaft and capital Beaux Arts tower design. It has a finely detailed limestone base with metal windows inset into the openings. The wall surfaces are kept simple and linear, creating a more modern interpretation of the classical style.

Frank A. Childs & William Jones Smith

1923

Equitable Building
Des Moines

The Gothic Revival theme is evident in this 19-story tower, with the vertical brick, terra cotta and granite detailing. The large terra-cotta roof lantern is a distinctive part of Des Moines' skyline and once housed the building's water tower.

Proudfoot Bird & Rawson

**Building
of the
Decade**

1920–1929

1928

Salisbury House
Des Moines

The Weeks modeled their home after the 16th-century King's House in Salisbury, England. Parts of the home are historic artifacts from England, enhancing the period effect. The interior public rooms are exquisite and the surrounding landscape augments the feel of the manor home.

Boyd & Moore and Rasmussen & Wayland

1930

Badgerow Building
Sioux City

The Badgerow Building is done in the Art Deco
style, which was becoming popular in the 1930s.
The ornamentation uses both the geometric patterns
of Deco style and symbols of Native American figures,
in an attempt to connect the city's past to its future.

Knute Westerlind

1932

Iowa-Des Moines National Bank Building
Des Moines

This is a sophisticated and understated Art Deco style building. The first five floors were constructed as a base to a 16-story tower that was never executed due to the Great Depression. The two-story banking floor is elegantly detailed with travertine panels and metal ornamentation.

Proudfoot Rawson Souers & Thomas

1935

Grandview Park Band Shell
Sioux City

This Streamline Moderne band shell seats 6000 in the natural landscape of a city park. The spherical concrete structure has the classic hallmarks of Streamline design—bold geometric shapes with a horizontal emphasis—that makes it look aerodynamic and in motion.

Henry L. Kamphoefner

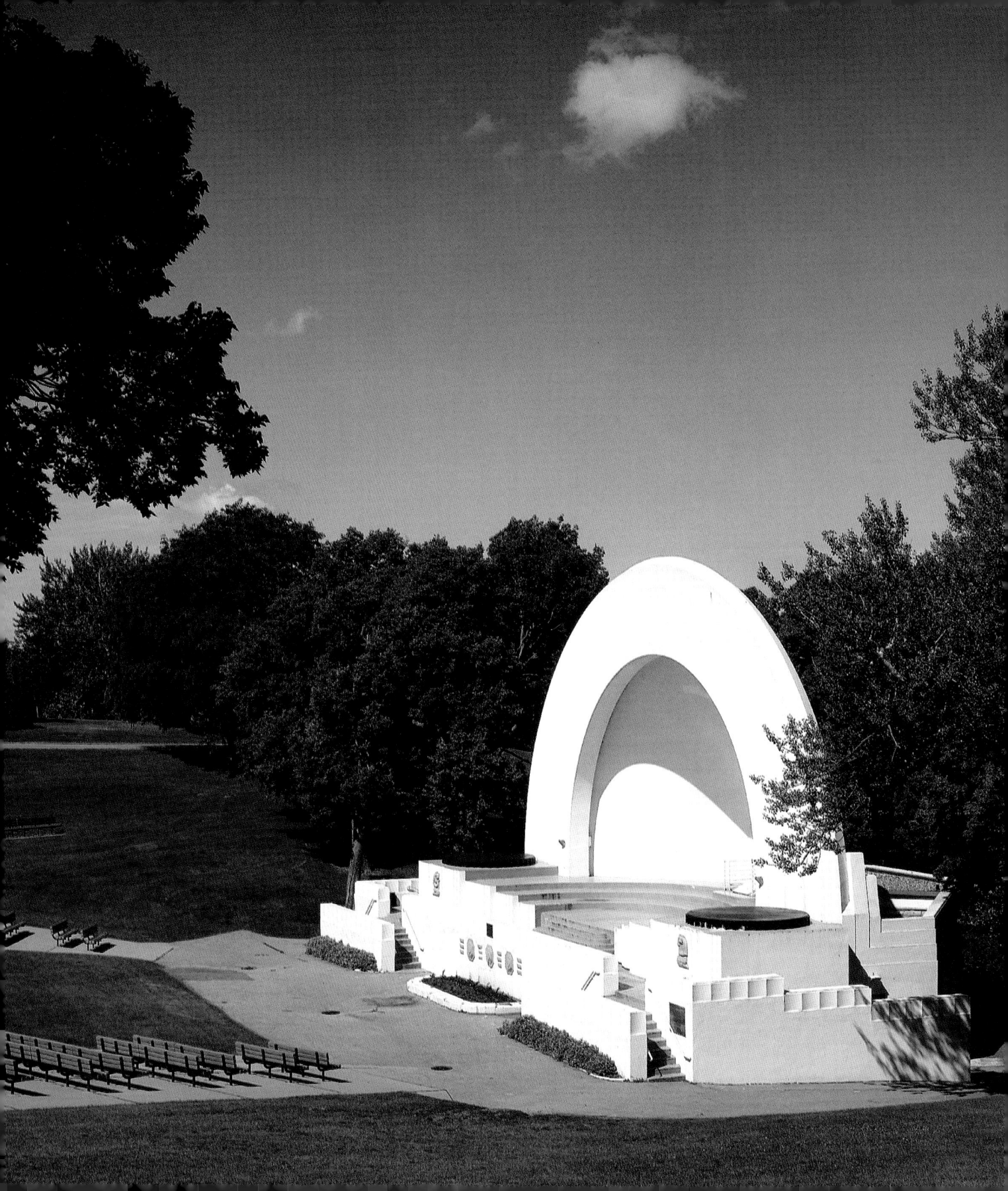

1937

Eagle Point Park Shelters
Dubuque

A remarkable example of Prairie School landscape architecture, the designer referred to the plan as "The City in a Garden." The park pavilions are constructed of a horizontal limestone similar to Frank Lloyd Wright's Taliesin buildings, appearing to grow from the ground.

Alfred Caldwell

**Building
of the
Decade**

1930–1939

1937

Earl Butler House
Des Moines

One of the finest Streamline Moderne houses in the country, it was widely recognized as a marvel of modern technology and construction. The interior borrows from Le Corbusier with a ramp used for vertical circulation rather than a stair.

Kraetsch & Kraetsch

1940

High School Auditorium and Gymnasium
Ventura

Constructed at the end of the Great Depression this project represents one of the last Art Deco style projects done in the state. The exposed concrete structure features the linear lines and geometric shapes associated with Art Deco and Streamline design.

Thorwald Thorson

1943

Julien Dubuque Bridge
Dubuque

This is an elegant expression of a long-span steel structure resting on concrete piers. While primarily solving an engineering problem, the gentle curve has a sculptural quality much admired during this time of form following function.

Edward L. Ashton

1944

Chicago, Burlington and Quincy Station
Burlington

This railroad station is one of the first Iowa buildings done in International-style modernism. It is completely stripped of ornament and relies on its form and materials to provide design interest. Its construction during World War II may have created the opportunity to eliminate decorative features.

Holabird & Root

**Building
of the
Decade**

1940–1949

1948

Des Moines Art Center
Des Moines

The Des Moines Art Center is a nationally renowned
museum complex, the catalyst being the extraordinary
Saarinen wing. It is a sublimely beautiful project that
defers to the landscape of the park, nestling into the hill
creating a front parking court and rear sculpture court.

**Saarinen Swanson & Saarinen Architects
and Brooks Borg, Architects-Engineers**

1949

Fitch Pharmacy Hall, Drake University
Des Moines

This is an understated, yet powerful example of modernist architecture. The Saarinen office designed an entirely new campus plan in 1947 and constructed this building as one of the first parts of the scheme. The auditorium entry is fascinating in detail and the skywalk between Fitch Pharmacy Hall and Ingham Hall was the first in Iowa.

Saarinen, Saarinen, Swanson and Associates

**Building
of the
Decade**

1950–1959

1950

"Cedar Rock" (Lowell Walter House)
Quasqueton

A fine example of Usonian design, it has a large open living core with a wing of bedrooms along a single corridor. The house is stylistically similar to Wright's projects from the previous decade, and has a fabulous boathouse that appears more modern than the main structure.

Frank Lloyd Wright

1951

Jack Lamberson House
Oskaloosa

The house successfully expresses Wright's interest with
the horizontal landscape through the large overhangs
of the low-pitched roof. A brick-clad kitchen forms
the core of the home with living spaces extending
to either side.

Frank Lloyd Wright

1955

Charles Medbury Hall and Oreon E. Scott Chapel, Drake University

Des Moines

A modestly scaled pair of buildings, the brick chapel is designed to sit in a courtyard similar to Renaissance church examples in Italy. The chapel interior is one of the most astounding modern spaces in the state, leading the visitor to a meditative experience.

Eero Saarinen & Associates

1959

Central YMCA Building
Des Moines

An eclectic modern building for its time, the functions of the structure are expressed as separate volumes clad in different variations of brick and glass. It maintains part of the original City Beautiful Movement with the large residential tower running parallel to the river.

Wetherell & Harrison

1959

Crites House No. 1
Cedar Rapids

One of Ray Crites' own homes, it has the purity of a structure done for one's personal use. The light steel frame and dramatic siting are similar to the Case Study modern houses from California.

Crites & McConnell

1962

Home Federal Savings & Loan Building
Des Moines

The finer of the two Mies van der Rohe buildings in Des Moines, the former bank uses sumptuous materials and exquisite detailing to distinguish itself. The siting both recedes from the street to create a forecourt and rotates to reveal a church tower behind.

Ludwig Mies van der Rohe

1965

American Republic Insurance Building
Des Moines

A classic example of the building expressing its functions—the open offices are at the upper glass ends with enclosed offices at the core, the glass level below the main box is the cafeteria and open employee space, the base houses entry and service.

Skidmore, Owings & Merrill

1968

Des Moines Art Center Addition
Des Moines

This wing was added to accommodate the larger sculptures and artworks becoming more common in the 1960s. Pei grinds the same stone used in the Saarinen wing into the cast concrete structure and uses the building to enclose the original sculpture court.

I. M. Pei & Partners

BUILDING OF THE CENTURY
1900–1999

1969

C. Y. Stephens Auditorium, Iowa State University
Ames

This is both an impressive example of sculptural high modernism and a strong commitment to the cultural life of Iowa. The auditorium is an icon on the Iowa State University campus and is skillfully designed for viewing a broad range of performances.

Crites & McConnell and Brooks Borg & Skiles, Architects-Engineers

1969

Maucker Union Building, University of Northern Iowa

Cedar Falls

The structure is submerged as part of the campus land-scape, creating a variety of spaces above and below for students to gather. The project enhances the existing campus spaces and buildings, while not trying to mimic their style.

Hunter, Rice & Engelbrecht and Brooks, Borg & Skiles Architects-Engineers

1971

A. H. and Theo Blank Performing Arts Center, Simpson College
Indianola

An intimately scaled theater composed of a minimal set of materials—concrete, metal and glass. The lowered siting of the project allows for access from bridges to the upper level or ramps to the main lobby. The interior lobby and theater are surprisingly warm and friendly.

Charles Herbert & Associates

1972

Iowa Society of Christian Churches Building
Des Moines

This is a well-executed example of late modernist structural expressionism. The concrete structure cantilevers out over the north and south sides of the building, with just a glass curtain wrapped underneath. The front plinth with the Miesian cross effectively creates monumentality in a small building.

Smith, Voorhees, Jensen

1972

Brenton Bank & Trust Company Building
Urbandale

A modern exploration of the expressive quality of concrete, the material is cast into sculptural forms around a rectangular roof structure. The project is a successful refinement of modernist ideas using the minimal material palette characteristic of the time.

Charles Herbert & Associates

1975

Ruan Center, Bankers Trust Building
Des Moines

An entirely cor-ten steel and glass-clad tower, the steel naturally rusts to a ruddy brown finish. It is a study in simplicity, with high quality minimal detailing and careful material selections that take a thoughtful viewing to appreciate.

Kendall Griffith Russell Artiaga

**Building
of the
Decade**

1970–1979

1979

Civic Center of Greater Des Moines
Des Moines

Part of an effort to give Des Moines a central gathering
place, the Civic Center is a backdrop to Nollen Plaza.
The concrete structure is carved away to reveal the
inside at strategic points, making the volume seem
less solid and dramatically lighting the interior space.

Charles Herbert & Associates

1982

Carver-Hawkeye Arena, University of Iowa
Iowa City

The primary concern of the building is the long span roof, so here it becomes the most expressive part of the design. The suspended-roof plane appears to float as you enter the impressive interior arena carved into the ground plane.

Caudill Rowlett Scott Architects

1985

Des Moines Art Center Addition
Des Moines

The final addition to the museum, Meier takes a more separate and sculptural approach than the previous two architects. The exterior white porcelain-clad panels are a signature element in Meier's buildings, establishing a link with early modernist ideas of design purity.

Richard Meier

**Building
of the
Decade**

1980–1989

1985

Des Moines Convention Center
Des Moines

This building uses a layered system of glass circulation
on a metal clad core to express the shift in the
downtown street grids. It is one of the few buildings
in Des Moines to embrace the skywalk as an integral
part of the building design.

Brooks Borg & Skiles, Architects-Engineers and
Loschky Marquardt and Nesholm

1986

Agronomy Hall Expansion and Remodeling, Iowa State University

Ames

A clearly expressed diagram of circulation and space is evident in the building's design. The material palette is sympathetic with the older buildings on campus without trying to imitate their style.

Bussard/Dikis Associates

1987

Coppola House
Des Moines

Once referred to by an awards jury as "a 1972 classic," the house stays true to late modern principles of straightforward geometric massing and simple openings. The basic functions of the house can be easily read by looking at the forms and the arrangement of windows.

Douglas A. Wells Architect

1991

801 Grand Building
Des Moines

Notable as the tallest building in Iowa, it has many elements of postmodern design evident—with historical references at the base and top. The tower is ordered on the classical system of base, shaft and capital.

Hellmuth, Obata & Kassabaum

1992

Iowa Advanced Technologies Laboratory, University of Iowa
Iowa City

This laboratory building is a collection of sculptural forms that is expressive of movement and energy similar to the aims of streamline design, but with a very different vocabulary. Each functional element of the project is clad in a different material from steel to copper to stone.

Frank O. Gehry & Associates and Herbert Lewis Kruse Blunck Architecture

1992

Forest Avenue Library, Public Library of Des Moines

Des Moines

Part of a successful neighborhood revitalization, this library uses a modern building language in a friendly and inviting fashion. The mix of materials and understandable building volumes add to the small project's appeal.

Baldwin Clause Architects

1997

EMC Insurance Building
Des Moines

This tower rises from a three-story base that relates to the scale of the street. The tower then deals with the surrounding context of other tall buildings. The building is clad in a highly efficient and sophisticated rain screen system.

Brooks Borg Skiles Architecture-Engineering

**Building
of the
Decade**

1990–1999

1998

Meredith Corporation Headquarters Expansion
Des Moines

An elegant addition to the earlier Meredith building,
the scheme creates urban space at multiple scales. The
project is integrated with the Gateway West development
and the park stretches through the building both
physically and visually. Beautifully crafted, the building
represents the ideals of the client.

Herbert Lewis Kruse Blunck Architecture

ACKNOWLEDGEMENTS

This book represents the collaborative effort of dozens of individuals making contributions of time, knowledge, expertise, and, of course, money. We would like to take a moment to recognize a few of these contributors.

For the financial support which made the publication of this book possible we would like to thank the members of the American Institute of Architects, Iowa Chapter, (AIA Iowa) who contributed to a special fund supporting our centennial celebration—their contribution over a three-year period was essential. In addition, we would like to thank the CNA Insurance Companies, Victor O. Schinnerer & Company, The AIA Trust (providers of the AIA-Commended Program of Professional Liability Insurance), the Iowa Architectural Foundation, and the Pella Rolscreen Foundation who made generous financial contributions in support of our efforts.

The nominating, researching, winnowing, and selecting of the buildings represented in this book was an arduous task carried out by a group of dedicated individuals lead by Jason Alread, AIA, and Matt Rodekamp, AIA; and including Wesley Shank, AIA, Professor of Architectural History at Iowa State University; Judy McClure, AIA, the former State Preservation Architect; and Jack Porter, the State Preservation Consultant.

Ultimately these buildings were selected from a nominated group of several hundred by a jury of esteemed Iowans including: Governor Robert D. Ray, the governor of Iowa from 1969 to 1983; former *Des Moines Register* Columnist Chuck Offenburger; *Traditional Home* Editor and former *Des Moines Register* Architecture Critic Eliot Nusbaum; former National President of the American Institute of Architects Robert Broshar, FAIA; and retired Professor of Architectural Design at Iowa State University Robert Findlay, FAIA. This group spent several hours carefully reviewing the nominated buildings to select *A Century of Iowa Architecture*. Their own personal knowledge of the state, informed by their own experiences with many of the buildings, led to a selection of works which are both beautiful and meaningful.

Finally, we thank the members of the Centennial Task Force which has guided these efforts for the last three years. This Task Force included: 2004 AIA Iowa President Geof Grimes, AIA; Allied Member Pete Bird; Jason Alread, AIA; Cameron Campbell; AIA, Matt Ostanik, Julie Severson and the staff of AIA Iowa, specifically the Executive Vice President Suzanne Schwengels, Hon. AIA; Director of Communications Jessica Reinert; and former staff member Maggie Laughead. These individuals worked diligently to keep all the contributors on task and allowed us all to enjoy *A Century of Iowa Architecture*.

Paul D. Mankins, FAIA
Chair
AIA Iowa Centennial Task Force